yukismart.com/b/60ab36

body

cuerpo

head

cabeza

face

cara

grow up

crecer

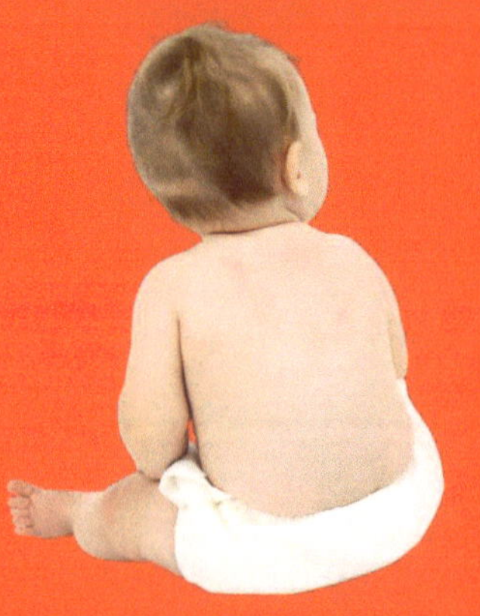

back

espalda

chest

pecho

bottom

fondo

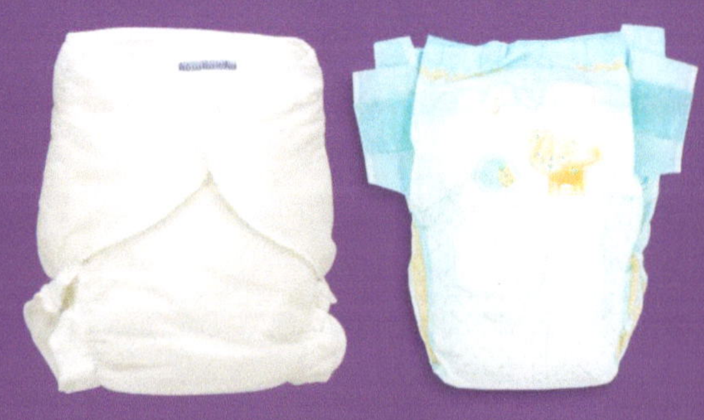

diaper

pañal

eye

ojo

glasses

gafas

forehead
frente
chin
barbilla

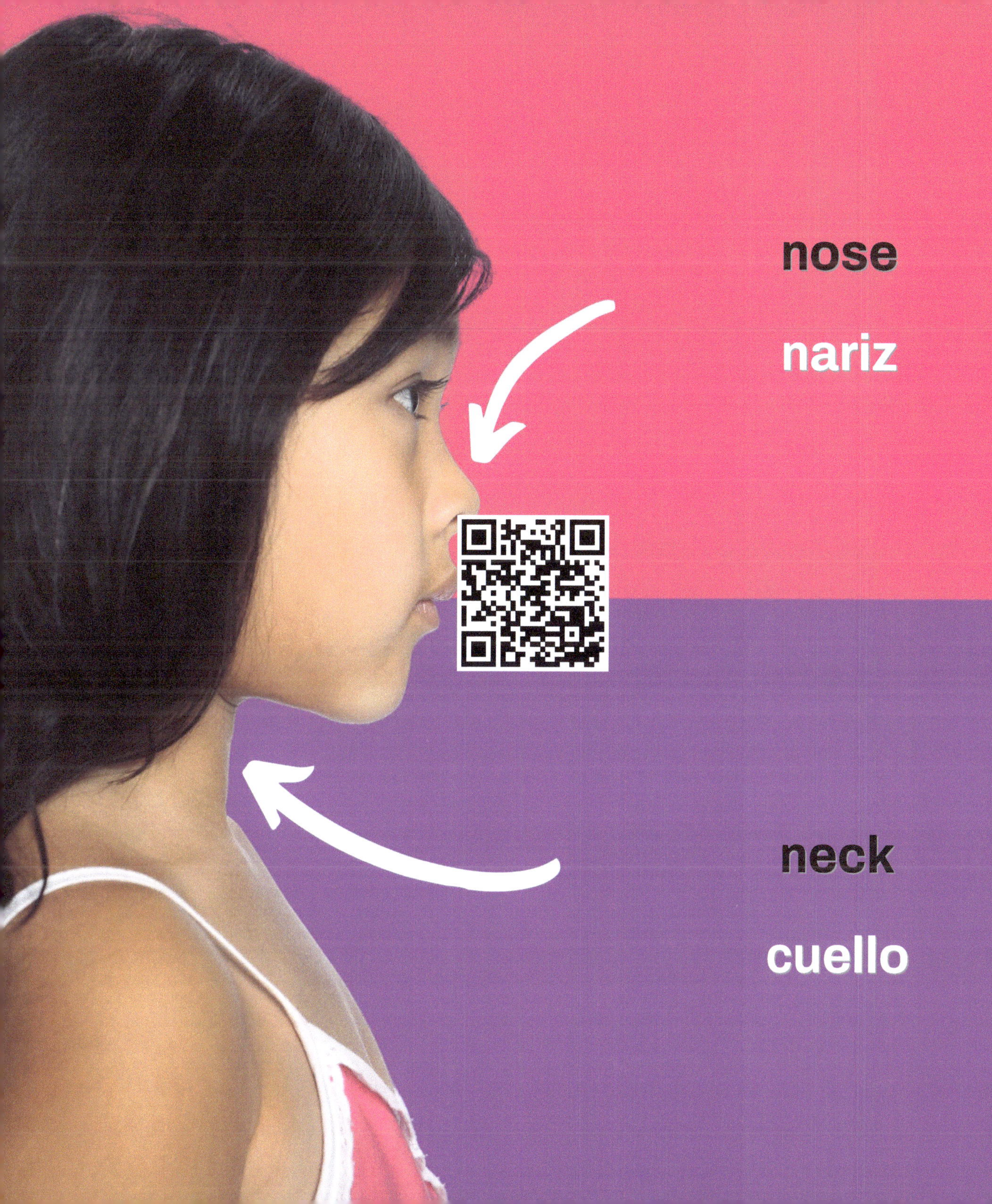

nose
nariz
neck
cuello

ear

oreja

cheeks

mejillas

kiss

beso

mouth

boca

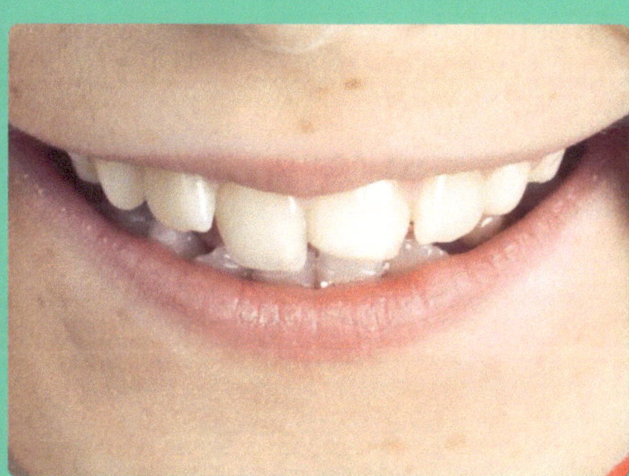

teeth

dientes

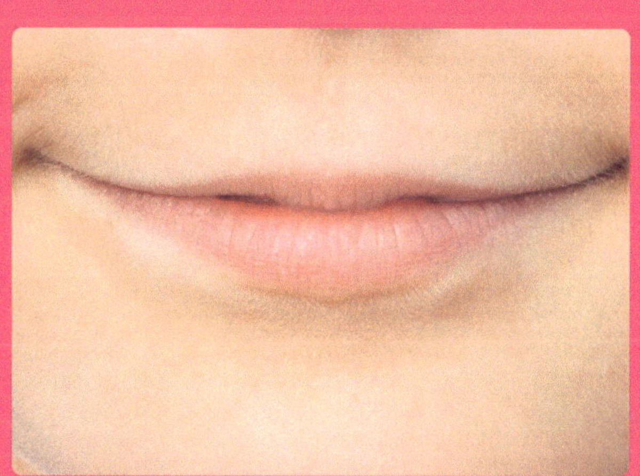

lips

labios

tongue

lengua

hair

cabello

straight hair
cabello liso

curly hair
cabello rizado

black hair

pelo negro

brown hair

pelo marrón

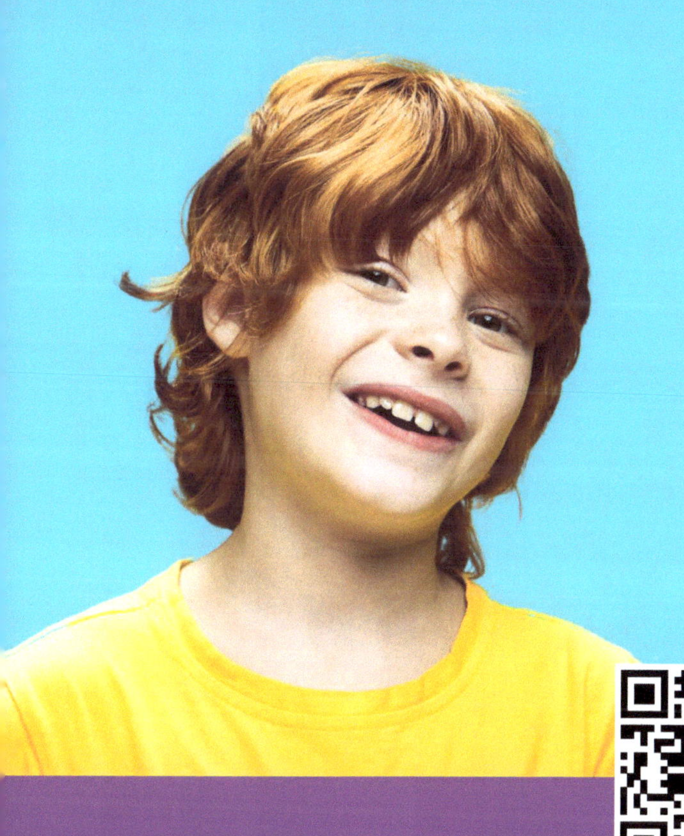

ginger hair

pelo de jengibre

blond hair

cabello rubio

gray hair
pelo canoso
bald head
cabeza calva

beard

barba

moustache

bigote

arm

brazo

elbow

codo

hand

mano

fingers

dedos

thumb

pulgar

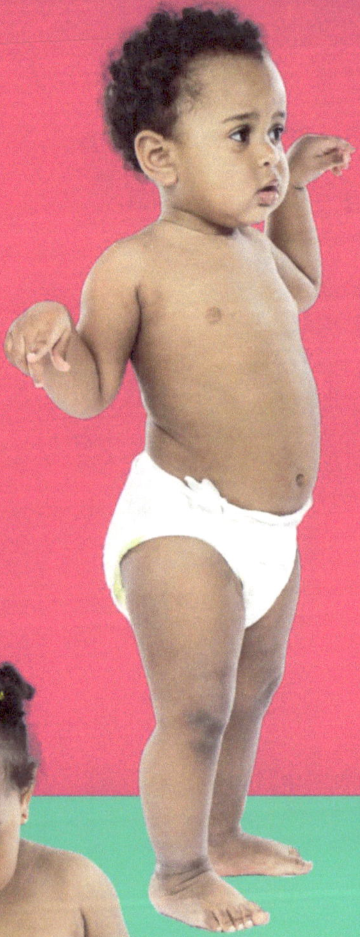

belly

vientre

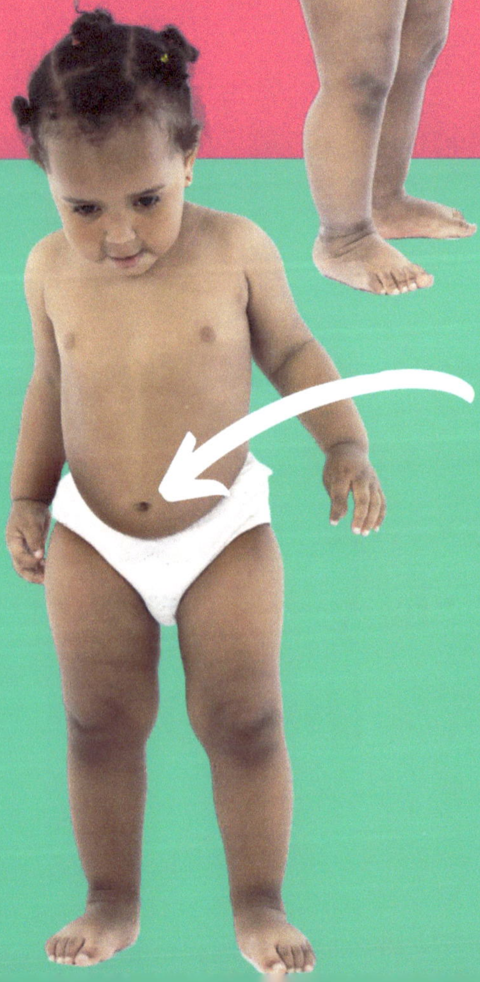

navel

ombligo

foot

pie

leg

pierna

heel

talón

thigh
muslo
ankle
tobillo

calf

ternero

nails

uñas

knee

rodilla

necklace

collar

bracelet

pulsera

hat

sombrero

scarf

bufanda

coat

abrigo

pullover

jersey

pants

pantalones

dress

vestido

rain boots

botas de lluvia

socks

calcetines

shoes

zapatos

mittens

mitones

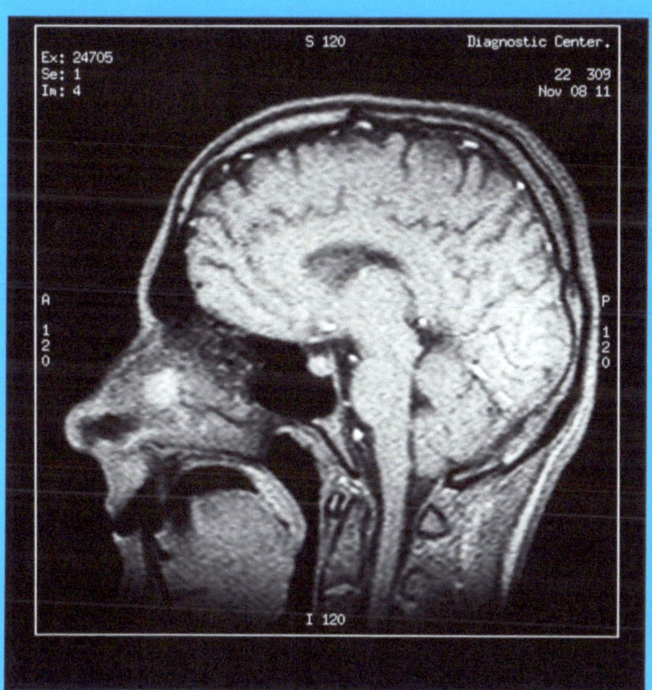

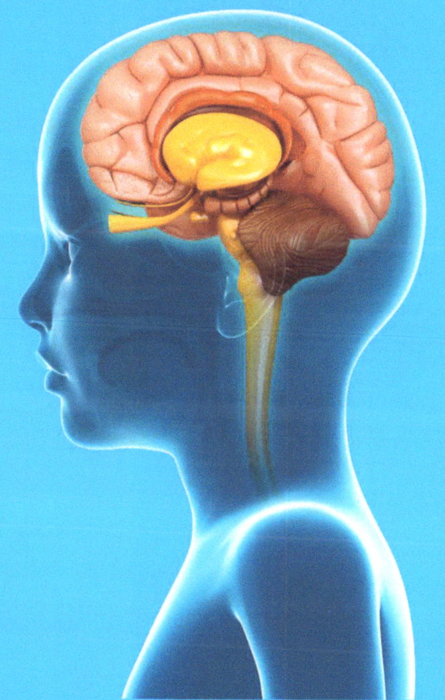

brain

cerebro

heart

corazón

lungs

pulmones

skin

piel

sunscreen

protector solar

sun glasses

gafas de sol

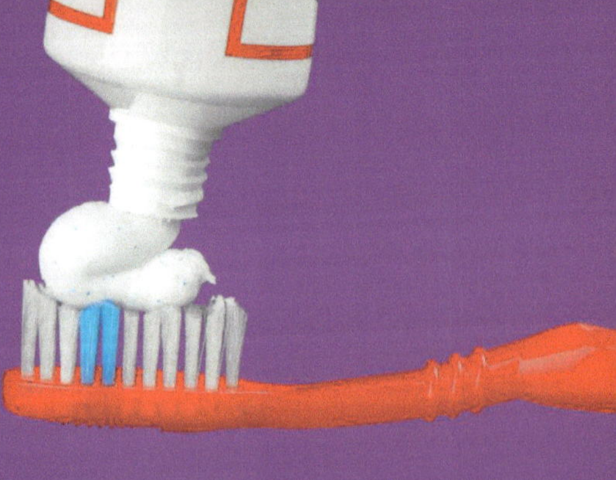

soap

jabón

toothpaste

pasta de dientes

toothbrush

cepillo de dientes

pain

dolor

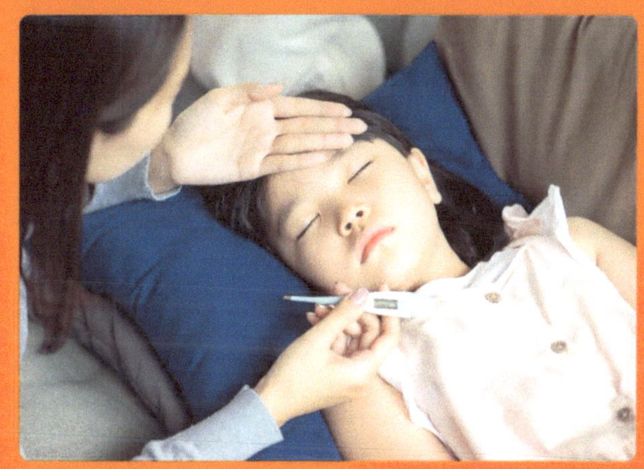

fever

fiebre

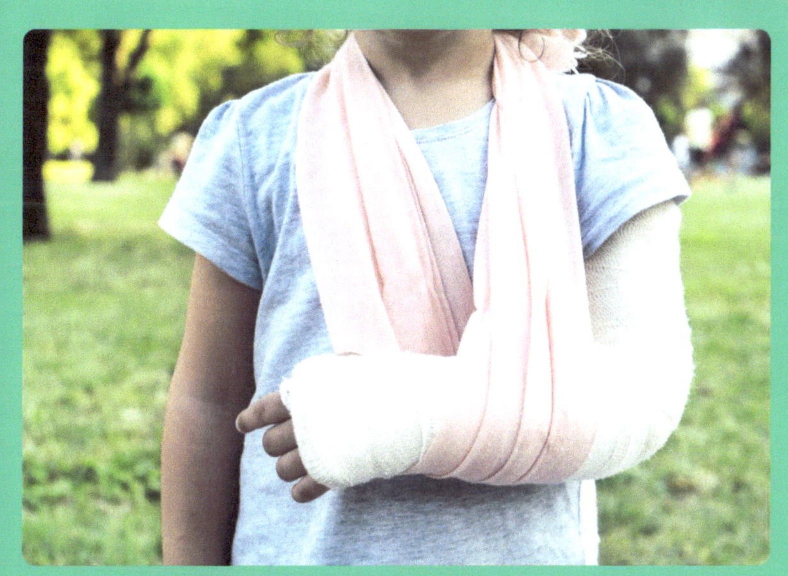

broken arm

brazo roto

sneeze

estornudo

cough

tos

dental cavity

caries dental

pharmacist

farmacéutico

medicine

medicina

hospital

hospital

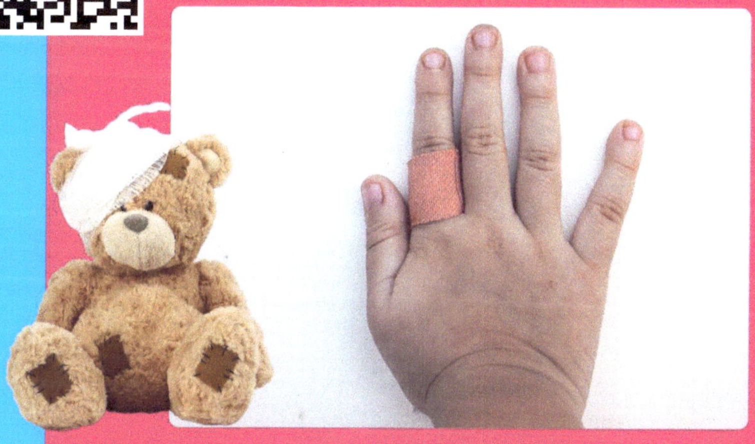

bandage

vendaje

paramedic

paramédico

fireman

bombero

firetruck

camión de bomberos

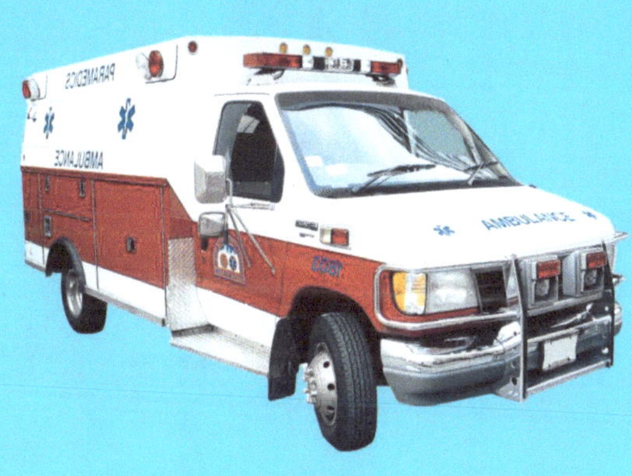

ambulance

ambulancia

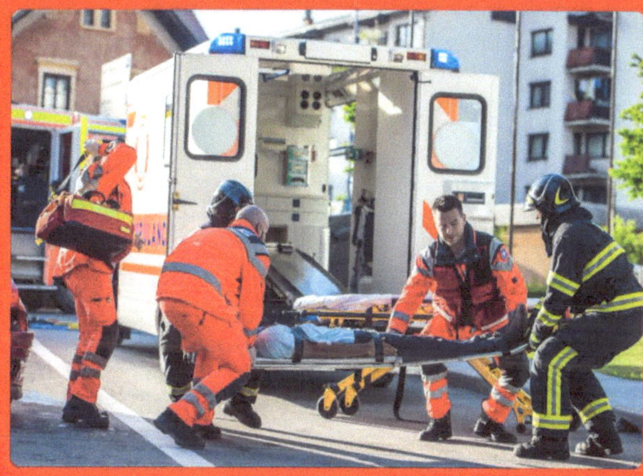

rescue team

equipo de rescate

helicopter

helicóptero

boat

barco

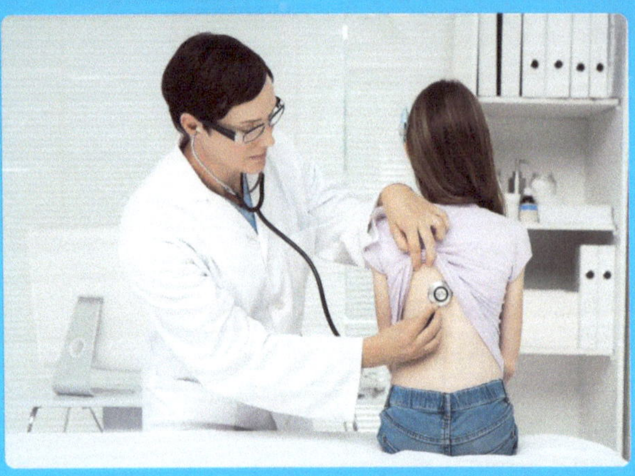

doctor

doctor

nurse

enfermera

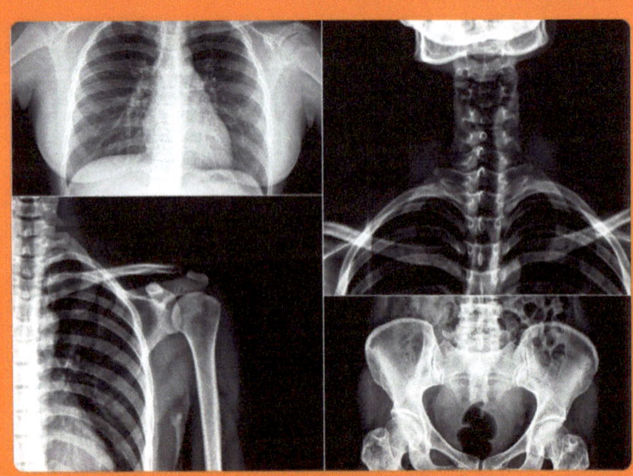

x-ray

radiografía

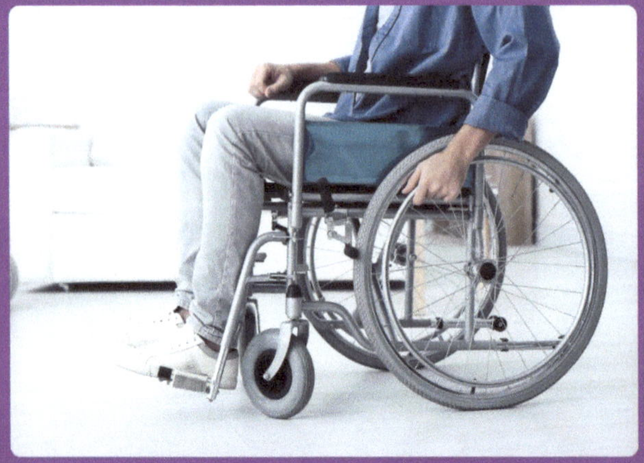

wheelchair

silla de ruedas

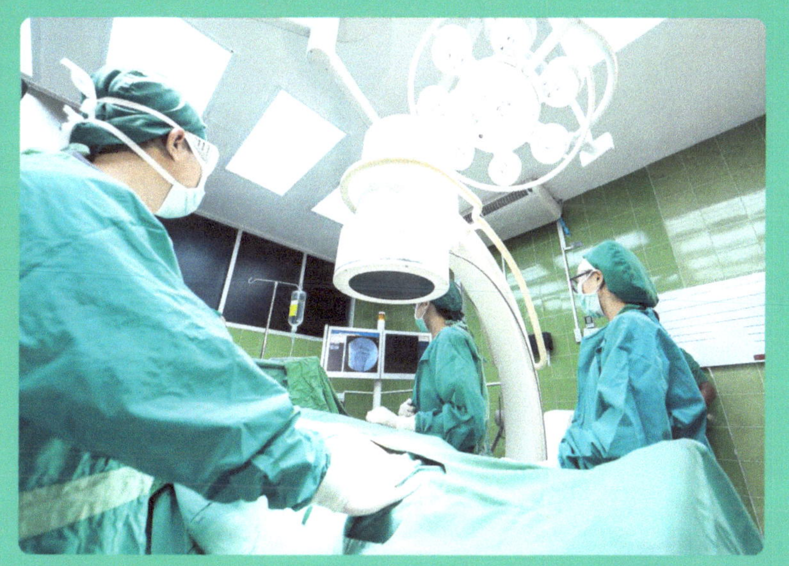

surgeon

cirujano

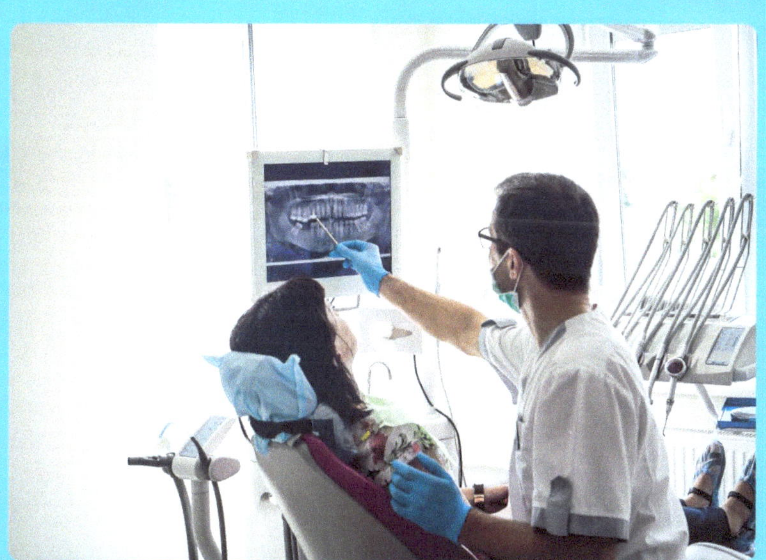

dentist

dentista

thermometer

termómetro

scale

escala

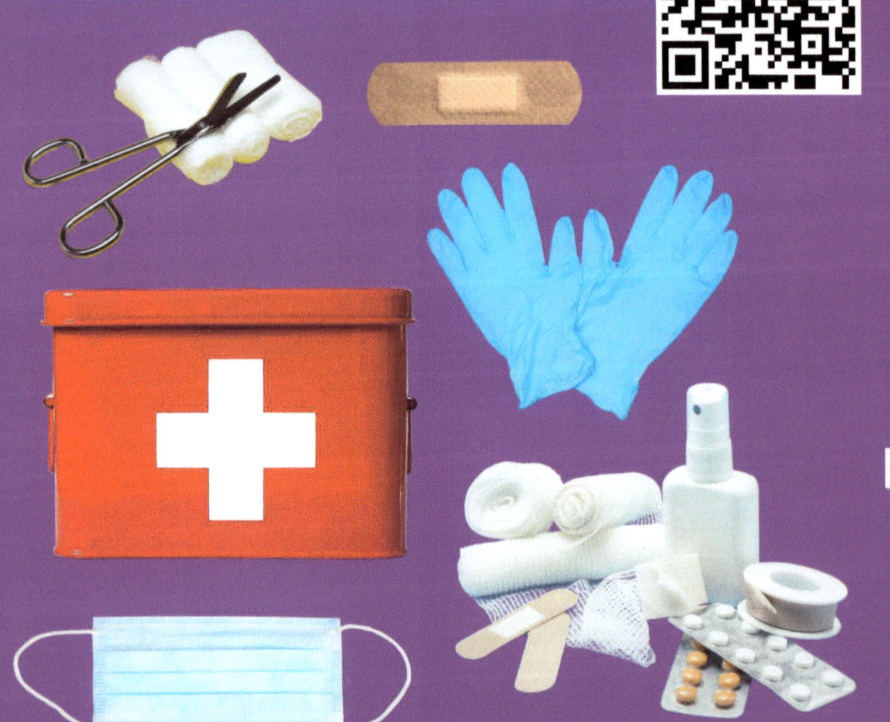

first aid kit

kit de primeros auxilios

vet doctor

médico veterinario

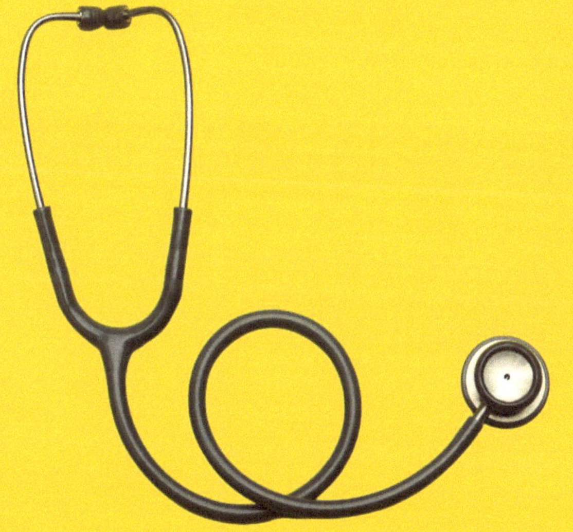

stethoscope

estetoscopio

dancing

bailando

basketball

baloncesto

soccer

fútbol

swimming

natación

skiing

esquiar

judo

judo

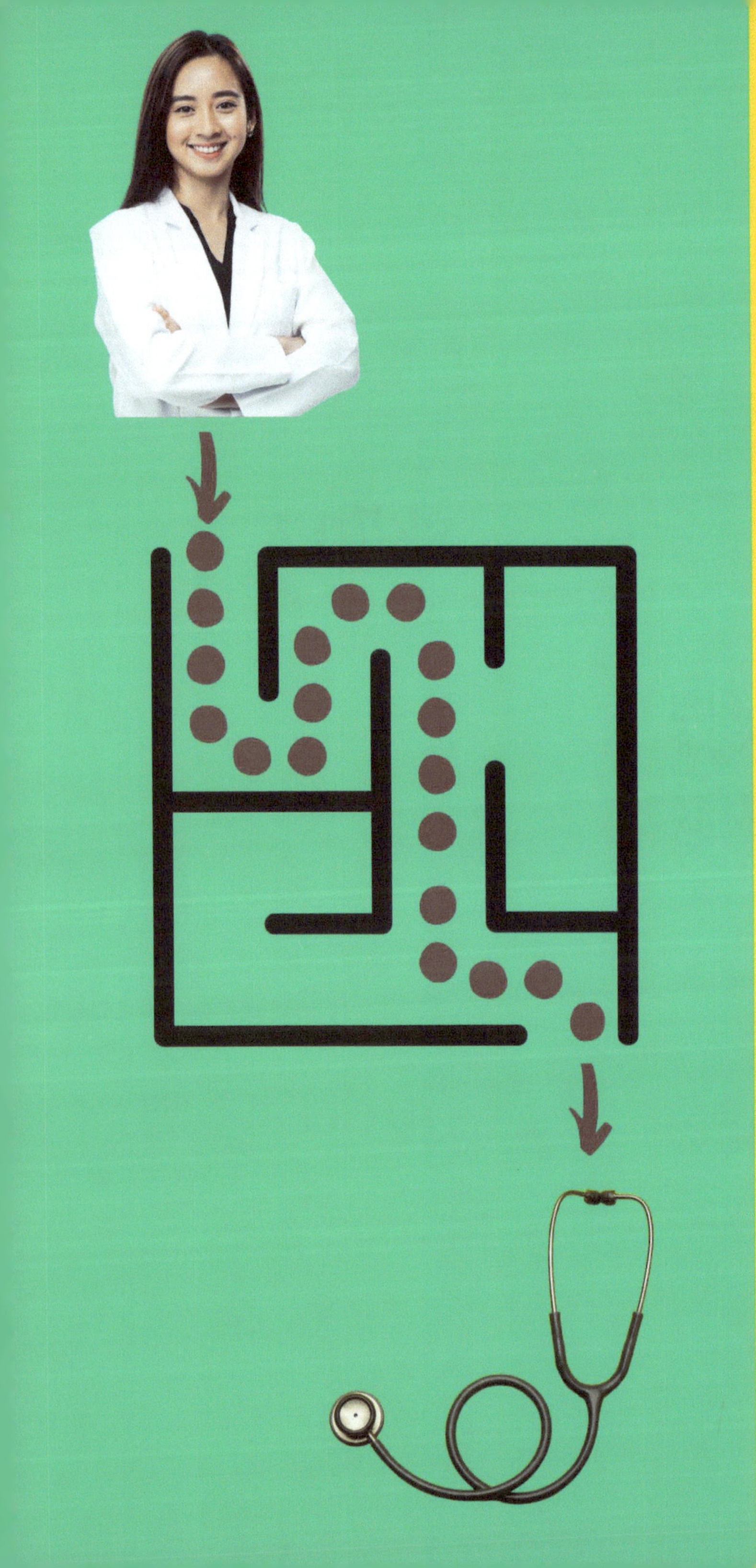